Journey through the Zodiac

An Artistic and Reflective Mandala Experience

By: Megan Ryan Walsh

Journey through the Zodiac: First Edition

All rights reserved © Megan Ryan Walsh
LCCN 2018903351

Published in 2018 by:

Inner Mandala Medicine
2110 Harrison St. Evanston, IL 60201
www.innermandalamedicine.com

Printed in the United States of America

ISBN 9780692071045

Acknowledgments

There are many people in my life that have touched my soul and influenced the person I have become today. If I address all of the countless relationships and meaningful connections, the list would extend beyond this page. There are a few people, in particular, that have greatly impacted the fruition of this book and have been influential in my healing journey at this specific time. It is those people who I wish to acknowledge here and dedicate this book to.

Lyz

My *soul sister*. I would not be on the healing path I'm on today if it wasn't for you and your Aries heart. You light the spark under my fire, and you give me the strength I need to stand on my own. Without you, I wouldn't have any platform on which to spread my healing, and this book would not be possible.

Tyler

My *mentor and teacher*. You opened my eyes to seeing the world anew by sharing with me the language of astrology. My lens is forever changed and I am eternally grateful for the wisdom you continue to pass down. I wouldn't have the means to communicate and express how I wish to heal in this world without your influence, and this book could have never come to life.

Danny

My *love and my guiding compass*. You continue to point me in the direction that I am meant to go. You push me beyond my limits, encourage me to do what scares me, and challenge what I think is possible. I would've been too scared to do the work to create this book if it wasn't for your example and inspiring heart.

A very special thank you to my editors and my mom.

Greetings!

I want to welcome you into this experience by first expressing my gratitude. Thank you for listening to that intuitive inner voice that ushered you to open this book. Thank you for putting your faith and trust in what I have to share.

I am thrilled to finally be able to share this project with all of you. These creations mean the world to me, more than I can express in words. This whole adventure began when I decided to combine my artwork with my love for astrology, producing one new mandala each Zodiac season. The concept was to allow the archetype to reveal a piece of its essential nature to me, and I would in turn create a mandala that embodied the energy I received. By taking those feelings and giving them form through a mandala, I hoped it would bring more solidity to my own expression and communication of those feelings and themes as well.

The project soon began to blossom and grow in pleasantly unexpected ways, and it took on a life energy all of its own. Each month, a new mandala continued to surprise me. Some of them came through with ease, while others came with much frustration and fear. Nevertheless, I always held faith in the natural process and each mandala turned out more perfect than I could've hoped. Throughout the growth of this project, I grew as well, learning so much from these forgotten friends I had acknowledged and welcomed back into my life.

This endeavor not only enhanced my understanding of the nature of each sign, but more importantly, it was an intense journey of self reflection. It gave me the opportunity to observe and feel the sensations of the season's energy expressing itself through me. A new layer of myself was brought to the surface through the unfolding of each new mandala. Looking at a deep piece of myself, now in front of me on paper, provoked the question of how I was carrying and relating to each specific energy.

The further I got within the process, the more I realized that I was giving a face to these living forces. The signs of the Zodiac are alive, and I interact with them on a daily basis. By condensing everything I felt about them into one image, I had given a new form to the unique way they reveal themselves in my life. Now when I need to sit, pray, or speak to them, I have something I can actually look to and hold in my hands.

I have learned so much about myself, the nuances and meanings of the signs, and the inner workings of the Zodiac cycle as a whole throughout this entire journey. As nature is our greatest teacher, this process was rooted in following nature's cyclical pattern and becoming aware of how that pattern operates through both my inner and outer worlds. Because of this, I've come to understand the language of nature and the language of astrology in a more holistic way than any book could have taught me. I've learned more about myself and my own cycles in ways I never foresaw.

My hopes for you throughout this book is that you will gain a new lens in which to view the world with. I hope that you will open your heart and mind to receiving the teachings of nature. By working through this cycle, I hope you gain some new insights into how you tick and how you can become more in harmony with the rhythms of life.

I suggest working through this book from the beginning to follow the flow. Read about each archetype and its position in the cycle. Take some time to reflect on the questions, then sit with the mandala and color it however you feel called to do so. In the process of working with and coloring the image, take note of thoughts and feelings that arise for you. Think and reflect on how they are manifestations of the sign operating through you. Or do the reverse; work through the coloring process, then go back and learn about the archetype and see how your feelings and thoughts relate. There is no right or wrong way, only what resonates with you!

When you've finished, you too will have put a piece of yourself into each image. Use them, connect with them, sit with them, and talk to them. If you are struggling with an aspect of yourself or an area of your life, revisit the mandala that holds the teachings you need and remember the feelings you felt when you first colored it. Let their wisdom speak to you through the image you helped bring to life.

Grant that I may be given appropriate difficulties and sufferings on this journey so that my heart be truly awakened and my practice of liberation and universal compassion may truly be filled.

~ Tibetan Prayer

Before we jump into learning about the individual signs that comprise the Zodiac, let's look at the wheel as a whole. What exactly does this pattern represent and where does it come from?

The first fundamental concept which needs to be understood is that the Zodiac wheel represents the basic pattern of growth and manifestation that all of life moves through. Everything in nature moves in the same cycles. All things go through a process of coming into awareness, growing and transforming, rebirth and evaporation. The cycle of the Zodiac is an underlying framework of nature. Studying and learning astrology is about adjusting the lens through which you view the world. This pattern is a fractal and can be applied to any layer of life - whether it's nature's seasons, the evolution of humanity of as a species, our daily life and lifespan, or any project we wish to bring to life. Once you shift your perspective in this way, you can begin to see the energetic patterns that flow underneath all of creation.

Why would we want to be aware of this cyclical pattern that runs throughout nature? Because we are a part of nature! None of us are separate from the happenings and rhythms of Mother Nature, although as humans we tend to think we are. If we can come to accept this basic premise and begin to pay attention to the cycles that life moves through, then we can adjust our lives to match the current flow. It's surprising how much smoother our life moves when we're not fighting the natural current of things and we simply ride the wave. That's not to say that hardships won't come; sometimes even the best surfers completely wipe out. But we won't be struggling unnecessarily all the time. We can use the current of life to help push us in the direction we wish to go. With this assistance of nature's cycles, we can travel farther than we might have thought possible on our own.

As above, so below. As within, so without. We are a part of the whole flow of the universe and carry all of those same energies and cycles within us. Astrology is a living language of nature. By learning this language, we can understand these patterns both outside and inside of ourselves.

How do we get the 12 different signs?

Fire
The Soul
Consciousness & awareness

Each sign of the Zodiac is a different embodiment of the powerful forces that are the four elements.

The elements are the basic underlying energetic architecture and foundation of all of creation. All forms both invisible and visible are comprised of these forces. They interact and dance together to create our world.

Earth
The Body
The physical container & holder

Each of these four elements manifests through three different modes of operation:

- Cardinal ~ *Initiating & Beginning*
- Fixed ~ *Grounding & Condensing*
- Mutable ~ *Changing & Transitioning*

Air
The Mind
The spirit & mediator between realms

Four elements expressing themselves in three different ways ~ now we have the twelve Zodiac signs.

Water
The Emotions
The womb of earth & source of life

Be sure to take your time with this journey, there is no need to rush. The whole cycle is a growth process, and each sign goes through its own individual evolution. You can't expect answers to come overnight. There is no ending destination or end goal to reach. We are becoming more in tune with nature, and nature does not move in straight lines. We are stepping into the realm of cyclical time. The path of our healing is not linear, but rather it is a continuing spiral. We will always come back to similar themes, and it is within the continual experience of our self reflection that we find our true healing.

Don't forget, the signs of the Zodiac are *living* forces that you are calling upon to help you throughout this cyclical journey. You're beginning the process of remembering very old friends. As you are re-introduced to each one, spend time becoming acquainted with it before racing onto the next. Reflect on them and keep them alive in your awareness as you go about your days. Look for them out in nature, at work, in your family and friends, and of course, in yourself. Once you make the intention of trying to see these energies, they will make their appearance known to you. They have a desire to be seen and acknowledged just like any person. You are welcoming twelve companions into your life. Have patience getting to know each one.

Focus on the journey, not the destination. Joy is found not in finishing an activity but in doing it. ~ Greg Anderson

A Moment for Prayer

In order to really get the most out of this new adventure you're about to embark on, spending time in prayer is necessary. Let's take a moment to come back into ourselves, back into the quiet stillness of our heart.

Why are you here right now?

From somewhere inside, a voice called out and prompted you to get this book. Whether you heard that voice consciously and bought it, or your subconscious manifested it into your life as a gift. Either way, you are here now. A part of you is asking to be initiated into a new period of growth and evolution.

Where is that voice stemming from? What is it asking of you?

Where are you in your life right now? Where is the place you want to be?

What are the ways you envision growth for yourself?

What is it you are hoping to receive from this experience?

What do you wish to manifest within your life and within yourself at this time?

Sit in this space for as long as you need. In the silence, pay attention to everything that comes into your mind. Listen to the thoughts and feelings, watch the visions and pictures that you see. There is an intention that is brewing deep in your heart and condensing its way down into your awareness to be acknowledged. All of the information being given at this time is that intention communicating with you, so take note of everything that appears in your consciousness.

When you feel ready, give thanks for what you were shown and come back into conscious awareness. Use the space below to write or draw any words, phrases, and pictures that came to you during that time. (There is more space for writing your reflections throughout this journey on pages 110-111.)

These are your visions and your dreams. These are the prayers that have now imbued the following pages with a sacredness. Hold them close to your heart and walk with them. They are the spirit that will guide you on your journey through this book.

Many Blessings,

The longest journey is the journey inwards of him who has chosen his destiny.
~ Dag Hammarskjold

Aries

March 21st - April 19th

*Do not worry if all the candles in the world flicker and die.
We all have a spark that starts the fire. ~ Rumi*

Finally, we begin taking our first initial steps of action towards the purpose of this book. In that prayerful place that we came from, there was an energy that sparked inside of us. It caused us to open our eyes, leave that place of stillness, and move forward. We felt compelled to take action and begin movement in our quest in manifesting what we desire. That spark and light bulb that flickered on in our minds, is the dynamic energy of beginnings, otherwise known as Aries.

Aries is the first sign of the Zodiac, and it is quite fitting that the whole cycle begins with the cardinal fire element. Fire is awareness, and when it's operating through a cardinal mode, our awareness is pushing out and driving forward. It is initiating movement and propelling the start of life itself. Aries energy represents the awakening of consciousness. It is the stage when consciousness is becoming aware of its aliveness and discovering itself as a separate entity. Since it came from this place of nothingness (and also everything, as we'll learn at the end of this journey), Aries has an innate drive to go out and develop its individuality.

In Aries we are discovering our identity, as that is the first part of ourselves that differentiates us from other people. As soon as we identify something or someone as separate from a group, they stand out to us in our minds. That entity has a whole new existence in our awareness. Because of this explosion of energy around the discovery of our own identity, there is so much passion around the individual self and what we are now capable of doing. That's why Aries can sometimes seem self absorbed. But this selfishness stems from an innocent expression of pure excitement at the discovery of the self.

Aries is energy in its most pure and raw form. It is the energy needed to create something from nothing. It's the jolt behind everything we start and that first push that causes a reaction out of us. In Aries we are simply waking up; waking up to our aliveness and waking up to who we are in our purest and truest form. Our whole universe began with the flash of the Big Bang, and everything in all of creation begins this same way.

Forms of Manifestation

Remember the feeling of the beginning of springtime. The time of year when nature is waking up again after the long sleep of winter before it. The birds begin to chirp, and little bursts of green buds begin pushing through the ground. We take action and plant our seeds in the soil, both literally and figuratively, for the year ahead. Those little seedlings hold within them the potential for the whole tree.

Imagine a newborn, headfirst out of the womb. His eyes opening for the first time, taking in his first breath, and simply experiencing his new reality around him. All of his feelings are instinctual and pure. Everything he sees is new and enchanting.

The hot, dynamic energy of creating fire by rubbing two sticks together, and the burst of excitement when that first spark explodes out of nowhere. Fire, heat, and light now exist and we can start working to build it larger.

The warrior, the leader in battle, charging headfirst into the fight. Constantly inspiring his fellow companions to do the same and sparking fires wherever he goes. He is not afraid to do what it takes to fight for his life.

Every morning when we first open our eyes and awake from our dreamy sleep. Every sunrise that ushers in a new day, a new beginning and fresh start.

Our anger. That feeling we get when we're frustrated at a situation of complacency in our life. That hot energy we feel that boils up inside of us just waiting to burst out. Realizing that we can use all of that potential energy in a healthy way. Directing it towards creating something meaningful and using it as a driving force for changing what is making us angry in the first place.

You are only given a little spark of madness, you mustn't lose it. ~ Robin Williams

Integrating the Teachings

Try for a moment to direct your awareness to this place of dynamic beginnings - all of the excitement and the newness to everything; the pure joy at the discovery of the world around you and your own existence! There are so many different ways this initiating energy can show up in our lives and so many different ways to feel this new excitement. By connecting to Aries, we are becoming more aware of what wakes us up and motivates us to move forward.

That burst of newness is an essential part to our existence. We need a spark lit underneath us every so often. Sometimes we need a slap in the face to wake us up. It's the initial drive that sustains our life. It's what keeps pushing us to develop ourselves. Without that forceful and instinctual energy propelling us forward, we would simply fall back asleep and drift away into nothingness.

Aries teaches us how to come alive and come forth into ourselves as an individual. If we want to survive out here in this human realm, we sometimes have to fight for ourselves. We cannot lose sight of our fiery spark and the natural instinct of who we are. We cannot move any further on our journey without this innate sense of self. Life is about experiencing our aliveness. We need that passionate warrior energy reminding us of the excitement of our conscious awareness.

The work of the individual still remains the spark that moves mankind forward.
~ Igor Sikorsky

Time for Reflection

We all need to be able to call upon our spark. How else are we supposed to move forward and go after what we want? We all have the ability to start a fire within us.

How do you embody this initiating energy?

What inspires you to get out of bed every morning?

Where in your life do find that spark that ignites you?

How do you generate energy for yourself?

Who are you in the purest sense?

Now remember those visions and prayers you wrote down before we started. Let's begin to take action and move forward with their manifestation.

What is the specific intention you can create for yourself that will bring these visions to life?

What are some initial actions you can take to start the manifestation process of this intention?

How does this intention spark aliveness in you?

How does it fit into your essential nature?

How will this intention drive you forward on your path for growth?

From a little spark may burst a flame. ~ Dante

I am pure.

My innate essence is untainted with a divine spark.

I manifest direct energy to move my life forward.

My drive pushes me to develop myself as my own person.

I am a warrior for my life and for life itself.

My instinctual anger is a stimulant for change and growth.

I direct this primal energy towards the evolution of myself.

I am alive.

Taurus

April 20th ~ May 20th

Be sure you put your feet in the right place, then stand firm.
~ Abraham Lincoln

Alright, we're awake! We've established our spark, that energy that motivates us to wake up every morning. We've gotten in touch with our pure essence. It's quite exciting, isn't it? But now it's time to put some tangible form to all that energy we've just conjured up. That consciousness does us no good if it doesn't have a physical vehicle through which to operate. This is where the energy of Taurus graciously steps in to fill that need.

As a fixed earth sign, Taurus is how consciousness becomes more dense and begins to root itself into this reality. Both our physical bodies and the Earth itself act as the body that our awareness needs. Taurus brings stability to the dynamic energy that we found in Aries. In this stage of development, we have the opportunity to process what is needed for survival and what resources we have at our disposal. Taurus gives us the time to make sure we feel secure in all of our basic needs before we go out and achieve anything. We learn to nourish and strengthen our physical vessels with nutrients and minerals, as it would not be wise to embark on a long journey without making sure our vehicle is functioning properly.

Not only does Taurus represent all of the concrete things we need in order to move forward, but it also represents what our character needs in order to stay rooted and flourish. Our value system and our self worth are the foundation for the person we will become. Our values are the soil for the garden of our soul, the land we're building our home on. We want to make sure it's the highest quality soil and best land possible in order to sustain all we wish to build in this life.

Taurus, at its roots, is simply the slowing down of our awareness. Here, we learn how to feel and embody all that encompasses our physicality. Through Taurus we develop our ability to take in the world around us through our senses. It is the pleasurable enjoyment of simply taking everything in. There is no deeper meaning behind it. Taurus loves to indulge in all of the delicious earthly senses because they feel so good to receive!

Forms of Manifestation

Imagine the middle of springtime, when all of the flowers are starting to blossom. The trees are becoming green and nature delights us with the lovely smell of fresh flowers everywhere we go. As each plant blossoms above ground, it is also growing its roots deeper into the soil in order to gather nutrients to nourish its physical form.

The root system of a tree. Growing deeper and deeper into the Earth, providing the stability the tree needs in order to grow tall. It continues to soak up nutrients from the Earth and send them upwards to sustain the life of the tree.

Simply the ground we walk on; the soil and sand, the rocks and gravel. They are always supporting us and holding us up on this rock floating through space.

Our senses, a blessed gift that allows us to soak in the environment around us. The simple pleasure that comes from tasting our favorite treat or breathing in fresh, crisp mountain air.

Protesters at a sit in. Like the strong immovable bull, they will not budge for anything other than what is right. They are rooted in a strong sense of ethics.

Our stubbornness and that feeling we get when we're being pushed in a direction we don't want to go. That strength we find within us when we firmly say "no." Learning to pick our battles and use this powerful strength to stand up for what really matters.

Our resourcefulness and ability to use our talents to help provide ourselves with the stability needed to survive.

Silence is a source of great strength. ~ Lao Tzu

Integrating the Teachings

Take a moment to observe the beauty of our whole world around us. Isn't it stunning? The fact that we are alive and awake on this planet, and in this body is so extraordinary in its simplicity. It can be easy to take for granted the gift of our physical existence, as we are often moving too fast to notice the stability it provides. Slow down every so often and think about that. When we can take the time to really appreciate the effortless beauty that life has to offer, we ground ourselves back into our bodies, and we are remembering and honoring all that our physicality brings. We all have an inherent worth and value within us or else we wouldn't be here!

Through Taurus, we learn to find strength from the reserves of the Earth. The ability to stay grounded and rooted, both physically and in our character, are qualities that are quite essential to our growth and development. A tree can only grow as tall as its roots grow deep. Taurus energy teaches us that before we can accomplish all the wonderful things we hope to in our lives, we've got to make sure we have all the fundamentals covered. This journey of ours is based is a physical reality and it would be in our best interest to slow down and really take in the landscape around us. Let's take a moment to gather the materials we have been given, work with them, and make them strong. Then we'll be ready to move forward.

Those who contemplate the beauty of earth will find reserves of strength that will endure as long as a life lasts. ~ Rachel Carson

Time for Reflection

We all stand rooted upon Earth, so we have that grounding strength within us.

How do you embody the energy of strength?

What is the fundamental set of values that you stand for?

How do you ground yourself and nourish your physical body?

Where do you find stability in your life?

How do you use your resourcefulness?

Let's come back down and root yourself in your intention.

Why is it valuable to you?

What value will your intention bring into your life?

How will it give you strength and provide stability for you?

What is your intention rooted in?

What are the materials your intention needs in order to grow and flourish?

And forget not that the earth delights to feel your bare feet and the winds long to play with your hair. ~ Kabir

I am grounded.

I am of the earth, formed of the same material.

I have an inherent worth and value.

With my feet in the ground I find stability.

I have abundant resources and am able to live comfortably.

I have the time to slow down and enjoy the simple pleasures.

I appreciate this planet we call our home, in all of its majesty.

I have the strength to stand firm in my beliefs and values.

I am worthy.

Gemini

May 21st ~ June 20th

We are shaped by our thoughts; we become what we think. When our mind is pure, joy follows like a shadow that never leaves. ~ Buddha

It feels nice to have settled down within the Earth, doesn't it? We have found a place of solid stability and have grounded ourselves in the physicality of the human experience. Now that our awareness is securely rooted, it's time to start moving! That original spark of consciousness, now in tangible form, needs a way to converse with the physical realm. There should be an interaction and a flow of movement between Fire and Earth. Consciousness needs a messenger and a tool to assist in navigating and perceiving its surrounding reality. From this need comes the first breath of movement, and the winds of thought and logic take flight. Now we enter the space in which Gemini occupies.

The archetype of Gemini embodies the growth and development of the mind. With our new found mental capacity, we gain the ability to gather, store, and compartmentalize undigested information. Up until now, consciousness (Aries) has been birthed into a realm of physicality (Taurus). With the formation of the mind in Gemini, we begin to exercise this new muscle, learning how to think and see the world through a logical lens. This function provides us with the necessary tool to operate and communicate between consciousness and the world around us. Our mind acts as the messenger and translator, relaying information between these two layers of life. Gemini also offers us the gift of language which we use to define our reality. Labeling, naming, and dividing the different things we perceive gives us the framework needed to make sense of this experience we're living.

Gemini is a mutable air sign which portrays the changeability and adaptability of the mind. Think of a radio receiver frantically adjusting its tuning in hopes of discovering every station in its vicinity. It is this innate sense of curiosity that causes the mind to venture off and learn as much as possible. It receives and delivers messages from both our outside reality and our inside one (which comes about with the initiation of Cancer). There is no difference to Gemini. Raw data is all he's concerned about and he flies with ease in and out of both realms. Such is the nature of the mind.

Gemini is the spirit of intelligence that is woven throughout all of nature. Up until Taurus, we are simply awakened physical beings. Gemini is the first breath of movement, an animating life force with the power to move and direct our awareness and our physical body.

Forms of Manifestation

Imagine the shifting season that takes place at the end of spring. More movement is happening everywhere, and we are becoming outwardly expressive and communicative in preparation for summer.

In nature, we see bees pollinating the flowers. Acting as the messenger, they assist beautifully in exchanging information between plants.

Picture the young child, who has recently begun talking. Always asking questions of pure curiosity: *Why? What is this? What does that say?* As they develop their young minds, their entire world is like a library full of new information to learn.

In mythology, Mercury was the messenger of the gods. Continually on the move, flying on between Earth and Mt. Olympus. He gathered information and details of life on Earth to deliver to the gods.

Look to the birds, the majestic winged creatures that can soar high into the heavens and descend back down onto Earth.

Watch the branches of a tree as they whimsically dance in the wind. Wisps of directionless air move them one way and then another. Their movement has no greater meaning or purpose, simply random, but nonetheless enchanting to watch.

Think of that excitement and drive you feel when you find a new subject to study or a new book to read. Our brain is giddy at the prospect of new stimulation and a mental workout.

Our focus and attention. Notice how sometimes it can be muddled and dull. Other times it can be completely scattered. We can learn to tune into that space where we are not caught up in the chatter of our mind, but simply observing and giving direction to the winds of thought.

No problem can sustain the assault of sustained thinking ~ Voltaire

Integrating the Teachings

What an incredible tool we were given to work with in this lifetime! We have ability to think, use logic, and piece together all sorts of information. Our brains have the capacity to store large quantities of raw data to pull from at anytime. It is really quite astounding.

For most of us, it's pretty easy to place our awareness in the mind. Generally speaking, the mind is the place we operate from as we go about our day-to-day tasks. When working with the mind and our thoughts, we need to have a clear understanding of its rightful purpose and place.

Think about how you feel when you look out to a blue and sunny sky compared to when it's gray and cloudy. Think of the energy difference between the clear and open vastness versus the more dull and foggy feeling. Imagine a calm and gentle breeze versus a violent hurling wind storm.

The air and our mind have the power to define our reality. It is the mutable nature of our thoughts to continually race around in our head. It is up to us to come from a more still and centered place, calming our minds and giving them a direction to go in. We need to make sure we are mindful and reign in our wild thoughts when needed. Without this constant regrouping, we lose our grounding in the whirling winds and end up viewing our whole reality as directionless chaos.

We keep moving forward, opening new doors, and doing new things because we're curious and curiosity keeps leading us down new paths. ~ Walt Disney

Time for Reflection

We are all animated with an intelligent nature and we have the power to direct this intelligence any way we chose.

How do you embody child-like curiosity? What invokes that nature within you?

What do you find mentally stimulating?

When do you enjoy a good conversation? Are you an effective communicator?

What subjects do you consider yourself intelligent and knowledgeable in?

What sort of language do you use to define your reality?

Let's have a conversation with your intention.

What is it trying to say to you and where is it directing your awareness?

What will your intention help you communicate out into the world?

What is the language that you are using to communicate with this intention?

Do you need to change your language, your thoughts, or how you talk to yourself in order to aid in its manifestation?

How does this intention help align your mind with the path you are walking?

Logic is the beginning of wisdom, not the end. ~ Leonard Nimoy

I AM CURIOUS.

MY MIND IS MY TOOL TO HELP ME INTERACT WITH THE WORLD.

THE DEVELOPMENT OF MY INTELLIGENCE BRINGS MOVEMENT TO MY AWARENESS.

I AM GROUNDED AND RECOGNIZE MY THOUGHTS AS THE MESSENGER.

I CAN LEARN INFINITELY, AS THE WHOLE WORLD IS MY LIBRARY.

I CAN BRIDGE THE HEAVENS AND EARTH, FLYING ON THE WINDS OF MY MIND.

I AM BLESSED WITH A VOICE TO COMMUNICATE MY THOUGHTS CLEARLY.

I AM INTELLIGENT.

Cancer

June 21st ~ July 22nd

Your intellect may be confused, but your emotions will never lie to you. ~ Roger Ebert

Now that our mind has learned to fly, let's calm those whirling winds back down for a moment. Let's take all of this new information and use it to initiate consciousness in a new direction. It's time to call upon a different kind of movement to life, one that pushes energy around into the swirling circles that nature moves through. Let's begin to lose ourselves in one of those spiraling circles as it spins us down into a new internal realm. It is within this space of immersive, cyclical dancing that we'll find the home of Cancer.

At it's root, the initiation of Cancer brings about the development of our inner emotional body. Our emotional sense is a nonlinear way of perceiving reality, in contrast to the more mentally dominated Gemini perception. This more subjective and feeling based way of receiving information cannot always be explained logically - and it's not really supposed to be. The development of Cancer is that of the inner child within us. What can seem to be an illogical emotion is really just that inner child feeling unsafe and vulnerable, voicing their concern in the best way they know how.

Since Cancer is the unfolding of our vulnerable inner world, there is a need to evolve boundaries in order to protect that fragile place within us. As a survival mechanism, we begin to learn to keep certain feelings and emotions to ourselves, only revealing them to those we can absolutely trust. Our emotional safety and security is the crab shell we build around ourselves for protection. Sometimes our crab shell may become too small for our maturing emotional nature. Think of a young person leaving home for the first time, venturing out from that place of safety and security, finding a new place to call home.

Our emotions can stem from either our external world or our internal one. Just like water, they have a reflective nature. Cancer gives us the opportunity to make time for reflection. If our gut instinct tells us to be wary about a new development, that's an important sign something surrounding that development needs tending to before moving forward.

As a cardinal water sign, Cancer is initiating the dance of life forward. Water is where all life begins, we all need it to survive. The gift of Water, along with our emotional nature, allows life to flourish and blossom. Now that we have established our consciousness, our physical body, and our mind, it's time to start living, experiencing, and feeling all that life has to offer.

Forms of Manifestation

Think of the beginning of summer. A time to relax and just be. We feel the Sun begin to warm the waters of the Earth and it reflects in the warming of our own internal waters as well.

Imagine a time when you were dehydrated. Remember the lively feeling of becoming rehydrated when you were finally able to drink water. Picture the Earth dull and barren from drought. Imagine the lush greens and bright colors of life that returns to it after new rain.

The womb of our mother. Those protective, nurturing waters that held us in a time when we were too vulnerable to be in the outside world. They allowed us the space to mature and develop until we were ready to share ourselves with the world.

The Moon, always changing, becoming filled with light and then releasing it all. The constant circular flow she takes around Earth, acting as our protector as she watches over us.

A crab retreating into its shell. He is always carrying that hard barrier on his back in order to protect his fragile body. When the time comes, he discards his shell that has now become too small. He ventures out into the world with no barrier to find a new home with room to grow.

Think about the qualities of dancing as a form of movement; feel the difference between dancing and linear walking. Dancing requires a certain sense of security within our vulnerability, allowing us to express the range of our inner emotions through a more cyclical form.

Our shyness, introvertedness, and fear of letting other people into our personal world. Our breakdowns and whirlwinds when we feel like our emotions are spiraling out of control. It's about coming to an understanding that if we take a moment to quiet the tantrums, we'll find a scared little child within us that needs a little comforting.

Unexpressed emotions will never die. They are buried alive and will come forth later in uglier ways. ~ Sigmund Freud

Integrating the Teachings

Think about how crucial Water is for our life and how every living thing on this planet needs it to stay alive. The inner waters of Cancer introduce the depth of feeling that flows underneath the seen reality of our human experience. With this depth comes the opportunity for us to become filled with emotion, moved to tears, and then washed clean. Our emotions, like Water, bring color to everything in nature. All of the ups and the downs, our high points and low points - those are what make our life exciting, beautiful and worth living. Through our emotions we can begin to feel our aliveness and feel the entire depth of meaning that is embodied in our earthly experience.

Through the initiation of Water, we see the wheel of nature set in motion with the circular movements that all of life dances with. These cyclical movements also govern our emotional body. Water flourishes when it is always on the move, as stagnant Water is unhealthy and toxic. Our emotions desire the freedom to move in any way they please. In accepting this desire, we allow them to fill us to the brim and then empty us clean, continually allowing us to become open to receiving new and beautiful feelings.

Our feelings are our most genuine paths to knowledge. ~ Audre Lorde

Time for Reflection

We all have our own internal water cycle. When we can be more in tune with that cycle and honor it for what it is, we dance more smoothly throughout our lives.

How do you process your emotions? What are your emotional triggers?

What causes you to get stuck in certain emotional patterns?

Who do you feel most comfortable sharing your emotions with?

How do you nurture yourself?

Where do you feel most safe and what does your inner crab shell look like?

Remember, we can never move forward if our inner child doesn't feel safe. Time to check in with our intention and use our emotional nature to set it in a new direction.

What feelings does your intention evoke in you?

What sort of color does it fill in your life?

How does your intention bring about emotional security?

How does it fulfill you as a person?

How has this whole reflection process made you feel so far? Has it brought up any concerns from your inner child that need tending to?

In the struggle between the stone and water, in time, the water wins. ~ Japanese Proverb

I am reflective.

I have an inner world which reflects the space around me.

My inner child carries instinctual habits developed in my earliest days.

I need to honor, nurture, and respect that part of myself.

I have a need for emotional security and comfort.

I deserve a safe place to develop and work through emotional tides.

I step out of my comfort zone and shell when it no longer serves me.

I feel my emotions to their fullest and allowing their release of me.

I am cyclical.

Leo

July 23rd ~ August 22nd

Fill your heart with the creative power to accept the past, decorate the present, and transform the future. ~ Osho

By the time we've reached Leo we already have a solid foundation, as each element is now alive within us. Our consciousness has become awake (Aries), we have built our physical bodies (Taurus), grown in our mind (Gemini), and developed a whole realm of substance within us (Cancer). Now we enter the den of Leo, who comes forth roaring and ready to share each of these elements with the world!

Each Fire sign brings forth a new awareness. With Leo we see the birth of the whole self. In the emotional waters of Cancer, we discovered a whole subjective realm of feelings. Leo now comes forth to share those feelings with the world. In this stage of evolutionary development, consciousness is becoming aware of its whole humanness and all of the creative power that comes forth. Through Leo we discover our ability to create. We come to realize we are our own creator and we have the power to generate our own love and light. Leo is our self-expressive nature. There is a need to express what we can bring to life now that our creative power is actualized.

This stage of new awareness focuses its attention on the full embodiment of our ego selves. It is only through our egoic body that we can animate and express ourselves in this human lifetime. Our ego is what makes us unique and differentiates us from other "selves" out there in the world. When we can accept and love our ego selves exactly as they are, then we aren't pushing against the natural flow of conscious energy.

Leo is a fixed fire sign, which represents the building and maintaining our own inner flame. That internal fire is what fuels our whole being so we can radiate that energy out into the world. Just like we need to constantly add fuel to a fire, our energetic flame constantly needs tending as well. It wants to be seen and grow to become the largest and brightest flame it can be.

Ultimately, it is within this place of Leo that we find our heart. Our heart is the one of a kind gift we've been given in this lifetime. Physically we need it for our survival, but we also need it beyond just its physical attributes. It is through the heart that we connect with the world around us. Our heart allows us to express and share what really matters to us, what our true meaning is, and who we really are.

Forms of Manifestation

Imagine the middle of summer. People are soaking up the outdoors and bathing in the heat of the Sun. Parks and beaches are full of friends playing together and having fun.

The young innocent child: *Watch me, mommy! Look at what I can do!* Playful and excited at the discovery of new things he can do and create, there is an innocent pride as he is coming more fully into his own self.

The performer on stage who eats up the applause and praise from the audience. Living in the moment, he completely embodies the song, the character, and the dance that he is creating. For as much as they may like the attention, performers also love to perform for others' enjoyment.

Envision the Fire itself. Think of everything that flame does in our lives and how it has impacted the growth of humanity. It is the Sun, the source of all of our life. Without the continual gift of Fire we would not be able to connect with the uniqueness of life here on Earth.

The feeling of being head over heels, weak in the knees, drunk and in love! Everything in the world is a little brighter, a little more radiant through the rose-colored glasses that love brings.

Envision friends around a campfire and the unique expressive space that creates. We share songs, dances, and pieces of ourselves with the group. Connecting with others through the heart and enjoying ourselves in the present moment.

Our pride and selfishness, our ego when it is out of control. Fire when it is out of control can be destructive. We need to come to an understanding that we sometimes need to tame our inner fire. A part of maintaining a fire is not only giving it fuel, but making sure it doesn't get so big that we can't handle it anymore.

Only from the heart can you touch the sky. ~ Rumi

Integrating the Teachings

Our heart reminds us that life is a grand performance. We were gifted with a uniqueness in this lifetime and we were meant to roar loudly with it. The flame brings people together and connects us with the hearts of others. A part of being a human means we need to continually add wood to our flame. By doing that, we are maintaining our own life and providing light for others as well. Keeping a healthy ego and healthy heart gives our soul the fuel it needs to do the work it was meant to do in this earthly existence.

Love motivates and drives us to become the best person we can be. Without it, we become dull and uninspired. We can become lost trying to find our way in the dark without our inner lantern. Love is the source of our fuel. We can find it from places outside of ourselves, but we have the capacity to generate as much of it as we desire from within. Building, feeding, and maintaining our inner flame is essential for our vitality. Look to the Sun: there would be no life here on Earth without it. So too can we look to our own inner sun to sustain the energetic layers of our being.

Leo introduces us to a new awareness that this life is fun and playful. Life is meant to be enjoyed and shared; we are meant to sing and dance our way to the very end of it. What is the point of coming down into this incarnation as you, if not to show yourself off and have fun while doing it!

The best and most beautiful things in the world cannot be seen or even touched - they must be felt with the heart. ~ Hellen Keller

Time for Reflection

Being human is fun. Being you is fun, and you're the only one who can experience it! We are all unique manifestations of the divine here on Earth. We all carry that ability within us to create love through the heart.

How do you embody love?

What makes your heart sing and dance for joy?

How do you use your power to create?

How do you express yourself and tap into your creativity?

How do you have fun? How do you shine your own light to inspire others?

Let's shed some new light on your intention. Get creative with all the different ways you can manifest it. You are the creator of your life, so bring this intention to light! Let it roar through you!

Does your intention bring love into your life?

Will it give you power?

How does your intention feel within your heart?

How would your intention express itself in your life? Within yourself?

In what ways can you begin to recognize your intention as a part of yourself and begin to express it to the world?

A loving heart is the truest wisdom. ~ Charles Dickens

I am creative.

I have a light that has the power to bring life into this world.

I am proud of myself and not afraid to shine.

My heart and the love I generate is special and meant to be shared.

My creative self expression is unique to this world.

I am courageous and stand fully embodied in who I am.

I have fun and make time for play within my life.

I connect with the world around me through my heart center.

I give my heart the fuel it needs to sustain me.

I am love.

Virgo

August 23rd ~ September 22nd

I slept and I dreamed that life is all joy. I woke and I saw that life is all service. I served and I saw that service is joy.
~ Kahlil Gabrin

Alright, we are now comfortable in our own skin. We've found our heart, what we love, and the ability to express that into the world. That's all fine and dandy, but now it's time to get to work. We can't let that creative power just sit around and waste its time all day. It needs to be put to some kind of service. We need to make sure that the love we generated is performing to the best of its ability - and sometimes that means it needs adjustments. It is within this desire for fixing that we find the crew behind the scenes of Leo's stage, and this is where Virgo loves to reside.

Earth signs are the holders for the Fire signs before them, and Virgo introduces us to the container for our new-found awareness of the self, our body of work. Virgo's energy is here to make our heart work in a practical way and fit into this world. How can we realistically shine our light in the way we want to? How can we contain it and use it here on Earth? These are the questions Virgo answers by bringing our light down from Leo and grounding it. In this way, we are putting it to good use not only for ourselves, but to serve the greater good of others. A part of the human experience is to enjoy life, have fun, and shine in our uniqueness, but at the end of the day we have to realize that there is a duty that comes with that. We have to take care of ourselves and others. We have to have humility and give back for the tools and gifts we have been given.

Since Virgo represents the separateness of the human experience (being in opposition to the unity of Pisces), it sees all of the broken pieces and chaos in the world. This is where the desire for healing comes into play. Our attention is now turned to self transformation by way of refinement and healing. If all we see are fragmented pieces when we look at ourselves and the world around us, we're going to develop a slight obsession with making it whole again.

Virgo is all about putting the pieces of the puzzle back together. It is a mutable earth sign, so we are adjusting the components of the Earth to our liking. We use this stage of self development to organize our life in a way that makes sense to us. This involves our daily routine of accomplishing necessary tasks, taking care of our physical health, and formulating a coherent system for making our everyday life run as efficiently as possible. Virgo offers us the healing we need, since being human means we are going to have to fix and adjust ourselves from time to time.

Forms of Manifestation

Imagine the transition from summer to fall. The plants are hard at work perfecting their fruits and vegetables for us to use. We put in a little more effort to get ready for the upcoming harvest season before we lose the long hours of daylight.

Look to the plants themselves, an intricate example of the Earth always at work. They take the light from the Sun, and through the process of photosynthesis, transform it into energy they can use and work with.

Picture the stage crew behind the scenes of a performance, working hard in the background making sure every little task gets accomplished - getting all the lights in order, making sure each musical cue happens, and putting every set piece in its correct place. We don't always notice it from the audience, but there wouldn't be a performance to enjoy if it wasn't for them.

The feeling of working on a puzzle of any kind. That focus and attention to detail that needs to be present in order to figure out how to fit all the pieces together and make it work.

Putting together your daily schedule and routine. What are all the little tasks that need to be accomplished everyday? What do we need to do to take care of our health so we're operating at our highest potential? All the little things that we do to make sure everything in our life is put in its rightful place.

When we do the healing work of trying to fix or better ourselves, examining the "broken" parts and analyzing all the options for improvement.

Our feelings of anxiety or compulsiveness and having an overpowering obsession with making ourselves and everything in our lives perfect. We need to come to realize that although the desire for betterment is honorable, we are already perfect just as we are. We cannot possibly "fix" everything we find wrong about ourselves, and we shouldn't stress over the things we have no control over.

We adore chaos because we love to produce order. ~ M.C. Escher

Integrating the Teachings

Without Virgo's attention to detail and ability to compartmentalize and organize, it would be extremely difficult to function in the human realm. At the end of the day we live on Earth, and there are certain things we have to do to survive on a day-to-day basis. Giving ourselves a structure and routine in our daily lives is extremely beneficial. Finishing all of the things we "have" to do in the most efficient way possible, makes it easier to go out and really enjoy life. Like all earth signs, Virgo helps to contain and hold us together in the physical realm, giving us guidelines and rules to live by.

It's a part of our learning journey to experience the division and chaos of living in a world that seems so disconnected on the surface. There is much beauty in that. However, it's easy to get stuck in the mindset that this separation is all there is to life. That's why self healing work is so hard - it's about looking past the veil of separation to see how all the pieces fit together. Virgo's place in the cycle prepares us for the shift in direction we are about to make as we begin our journey back home to becoming whole. When we activate our Virgo nature within us, we walk the path of the healer and begin to mend the forgotten pieces of our soul.

Virgo bestows us with the gift of seeing the "brokenness" within all aspects of life. With that gift comes the responsibility and intention that we do the necessary work to try and put the pieces back together. Through Virgo, we come to learn that we are just one puzzle piece, intricately entangled within a greater system of nature. The healing we provide for ourselves can become a reflection of how we heal others, and nature, as a whole.

This is the very perfection of a man, to find out his own imperfections. ~ St. Augustine

Time for Reflection

We are all a part of this intricate system of nature. We each have a place, a role to play, and a unique service to offer. We all have healing work that needs to be done.

How do you embody this healing nature? Where do you find your healing?

In what ways are you being of service to others, to Mother Earth, and to all of her inhabitants?

How do you work with all of the pieces and components of you life?

What is your routine you've created to successfully navigate your heart through this life? What does that "perfect" routine look like, if you're not there yet?

How do you take care of your physical health?

Let's work on that intention so it can practically function for you.

How will your intention bring you healing?

What piece does it fill in the whole of you?

How can you "perfect" it to make it work in a more efficient and practical way?

Does it bring you a sense of humility, taming the flames of your ego?

How can you use this intention to be of service to all of life? Does it promote a healing for the planet as a whole?

Only a person who has passed through the gate of humility can ascend to the heights of the spirit. ~ Rudolf Steiner

I am healing.

I am one piece of the intricate system of nature and mother earth.

My duty is to give back to others and care for this planet.

I heal and tend to the health of my ever changing physical body.

I take the light from my heart and put it to work, creating a service.

I bring structure and order to my daily life and habits.

I walk the path of the healing journey, returning home to wholeness.

I am perfectly imperfect.

I am working.

Libra

September 23rd ~ October 22nd

The beauty of a sunset is shared by all human beings.
~ J. Krishnamurti

We've made it to the halfway point of our cycle! That separate spark of Aries has now grown through the first six stages of development, becoming a fully functioning self in this earthly realm. Since we're on a cyclical path, the only place we can go for the remainder of the journey is circling back around to where we began. It is within this shifting of directions that we see the scales tip, ushering in an equilibrium to the universe. This balancing force holding these cosmic scales is our dear friend, Libra.

This stage in the evolutionary process ushers in the need for a state of symmetry. Everything in the universe needs to stay in balance and will consistently work to maintain it. What goes up, must come down. Like all cardinal signs, Libra initiates consciousness in a new direction, changing the facing of the second half of our journey back to where we came from. In Virgo, consciousness completely integrated itself into the working system of human existence, but Libra politely steps in to remind us of another side to things. We can't get too caught up in ourselves or our experience. There's a lot more we can learn about this life by looking outside of ourselves.

Since Libra is an air sign, it deals in the realm of our mind. It allows us to thoughtfully integrate another lens through which we view our world. Our mental capacity always deals in dualities, and through Libra our mind begins to conceptualize oppositions. I am me and you are you, we both have our own different thoughts and feelings. We also begin to see the opposing side of all of the energies developed within ourselves through the first half of the journey. We learn to see our reality not just through our own eyes and preconceptions, but through the eyes and ideas of others.

This is why Libra is representative of our relationships and partnerships. In Aries we developed who we are as an individual. To balance that out, we need to take into consideration other people in our life and the lessons we learn from hearing a different side of things. We begin to get a more complete picture of ourselves, as relationships offer up that mirror through which we can see ourselves more clearly. We can never fully understand ourselves without understanding our relationships. Through this initiation of oppositions, Libra is teaching us how to compromise. This way we avoid unnecessary conflict and maintain stability and balance in our lives. Ultimately, it is the new desire for finding equilibrium that is leading us back down the path to wholeness.

Forms of Manifestation

Remember the beginning of the fall season, when we see a slight shift in nature as the trees begin to change colors. We have hit the Fall Equinox, the scale has tipped and the hours of darkness become longer than the daylight.

It's now harvest season and we reap the benefits of the seeds we planted in the spring. We enjoy the pleasures of our fruits and vegetables. We share with our neighbors in exchange for the foods we did not harvest, living in reciprocity and both benefitting from abundance.

The sunset, a time in the cycle of our day when we shift into the darker half. Nature delights us with aesthetically pleasing colors that radiate from this lovely scene.

Our breath and the constant exchange of carbon dioxide for oxygen. We are always in a give-and-take relationship with life on Earth.

Our relationships and when we're interacting with our friends or acquaintances. The growth that comes when we realize there are more views and opinions out there than our own. The partnerships we develop as we learn to see ourselves through different lenses.

The act of looking in a mirror. We could go for days without seeing a reflection of ourselves and have a pretty good idea of what we might look like. But that mirror gives us a clearer picture, and sometimes we realize we've actually had food stuck in our teeth all day.

Our indecisiveness when we can see both sides of a situation so clearly that we can't choose either one. The times we don't disturb a seemingly harmonious situation with our own desires. Although we need to consider others, we cannot forget ourselves. There is almost always a way to find compromise between authentic individuals.

Everything that irritates us about others can lead us to an understanding of ourselves.
~ Carl Jung

Integrating the Teachings

We must honor all opposites and all relations in our lives; they provide our universe with the equilibrium and stability it requires. Be grateful for different viewpoints, different perspectives, and different people. The opportunity to learn about yourself through the lens of another is the only way to become truly whole. If we really want to understand who we *are*, then we have to understand that there are things we are *not*. Sometimes these outside forces that we can't control are going to throw off our natural balance. We then have a better understanding of what we need to bring us back into balance that we may not have known otherwise.

We are all dependent on each other. Yes, we became a self through the energy of Aries. It's always important to remember who we are and to remember our true self. But we are not alone. We don't have to live fighting for our own survival all the time. When our attention is placed too heavily on the Aries within us, only looking out for our own best interest, we lose harmony within our relationships and our lives as a whole. We are not going to be able to move forward without an understanding that we share most aspects of our life with others.

Libra gifts us with the ability to find harmony within our lives. We share Earth and this existence with a whole world full of others, all with different wants and desires. If we treat others with equality and fairness, then we're working towards honoring everyone's happiness and satisfaction through the beauty of compromise. Our happiness does not come at the expense of another. Mother Earth, too, shares her gifts with us and there is plenty to go around for everyone. When we can live in reciprocity with our fellow humans and the Earth, then we have understood Libra's teachings.

Reciprocity is a matter of keeping the gift in motion through self-perpetuating cycles of giving and receiving. ~ Robin Wall Kimmerer

Time for Reflection

We are all working towards our own internal balance. We all have the ability to learn from our reflections.

How do you maintain balance within your life?

When do you feel perfectly harmonious within yourself?

How do you relate to others?

What do you seek from others in a relationship? What do you lack that others can teach you?

Putting yourself in someone else's shoes, how do you think others see you?

Time to learn something new about your intention and see another side to it.

Does your intention bring balance and harmony into your life?

Are there any problems or issues that might arise from it that would affect your balance?

Does it affect other people at all?

Is there something you need to shift within yourself in order to maintain balance?

How can you share this intention with someone else and learn something new about it?

Your hand opens and closes, opens and closes. If it were always a fist or always stretched open, you would be paralysed. Your deepest presence is in every small contracting and expanding, the two as beautifully balanced and coordinated as birds' wings. ~ Rumi

I am balanced.

I am in harmony with myself and the world around me.

In honoring my reflections, I begin to understand my wholeness.

I see another side to life through my interactions with others.

My relationships bring about needed opposition into my life.

I embrace compromise as a way of maintaining equilibrium.

I live in reciprocity with all forms of life.

I am, and I am not.

Scorpio

October 23rd ~ November 21st

The cave you fear to enter holds the treasure you seek.
~ Joseph Campbell

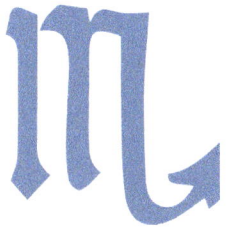

So we finally shared parts of ourselves with other people! We were introduced to new ways of thinking and were shown the other side of the coin. In the process we figured out how to maintain harmony between ourselves and the outside world. It feels so peaceful, doesn't it? Let's just stay right here. No need to disrupt the balance, we'll simply bask in this aesthetically pleasing life. Nice try, Libra. As nice as that may be, our consciousness needs to keep moving and evolving. Sometimes that means tipping one of the scales and sending them wildly out of balance. This blindsided attack comes out of the darkness where Scorpio hiding.

Up until this point in the cycle, consciousness has had it pretty easy. Sure, we've experienced challenges that come with growth, but now it's time to cut the crap and get real. Let's talk life and death. Let's go to those places everyone wants to avoid and talk about those feelings no one wants to deal with. It's time to get raw, go deep, and dive all in. Scorpio has no problem pushing us down there with a pleasurable ease. Mystery, death, and the unknown are all the realms we're uncovering now. The journey back home takes us on a route that involves traveling further and further outside of ourselves. Scorpio shatters our known reality and for a moment, introducing us to the place just beyond the veil of this seen human existence.

Throughout this whole journey, each sign brought us new lessons and layers that we have been adding to ourselves and our truth. Scorpio asks us to feel that core essence again and peels back the layers of our unconscious for us to access it. When we begin to dissolve those boundaries we placed on ourselves and on our lives, we realize there's a lot more depth to our surface-level awareness of the world. There's a deeper connectedness to all things and a mystery to life that we may never know. These experiences make us question what we thought we knew and who we thought we were. No one ever comes back from a near death experience as the same person. Something profound strikes us. We transform, becoming more aligned with our truth.

Scorpio can be found hidden within the depths of our own inner waters or within the depths of another. Scary and uncharted territory, like being shoved into a pitch black room with no flash light. Operating as a fixed water sign, Scorpio drags us down to the depths of the oceans and freezes the emotional waters within us. We shiver uncomfortably as we are forced to look at what's now frozen, what was lurking beneath which we chose to ignore. Feelings and emotions that were previously hidden are now brought to the surface. The only way to change our own darkness is by bringing them into the light of our conscious awareness.

Forms of Manifestation

Picture the middle of the fall season when we begin to see more death all around us in nature. The leaves are rapidly losing their lively green colors. We see them drying, shriveling, and falling off the tree, leaving nothing but the bare skeleton.

Imagine the depths of the ocean, a still dark lake, or the eerie feeling of seeing something that was once alive frozen in ice. Think of the sort of emotions that are brought up inside of us when we experience Water operating in this way.

Simply, the darkness. In the daylight we can see all that is around us. But in the dark, we cannot see what we once could. There is an uncertainty that develops. What is out there now? The place that was once known to us is now shrouded in a veil of mystery.

Our intimate relationships and the vulnerability that is required when in that space. Being that close to another soul requires us to open up layers of ourselves that maybe we didn't even know we had. We need to be 100% real and completely honest if we want the partnership to succeed. Since others operate as that mirror, the further and deeper we get to know someone else, the deeper we end up diving into ourselves as well.

The feeling of being frightened and too scared to move forward. In contrast, those times when we take a dive into the unknown, pushing forward full force, and giving our all no matter what the outcome. When we work toward overcoming our fears, that is when we can tap into our power.

Those moments of complete loss, suffering, and pain that take hold of us and drag us down. Those times we are swallowed up in our darkness, unable to find the light. Realizing that we have the power to use these ultimate emotional lows and dark moments for profound transformation. They are an unavoidable place we must pass on this cyclical journey.

He who has overcome his fears will truly be free. ~ Aristotle

Integrating the Teachings

There is great power in death and transformation. Anything that wasn't our core truth is now dead and what remains is only what matters. By opening up our layers and becoming vulnerable to the mystery, we open ourselves to that brief connection with Source. We are reminded that there is more to this human existence than we can see and perceive with our mind. It can be felt deep inside of us and in all those places we fear.

Through Taurus we learned how to build and fortify our boundaries in order to give us strength. We planted our roots deep in the soil of our values, so that we may never become uprooted. Taurus teaches valuable and fundamental lessons, but we never want to become too stuck in our ways. The balancing energy of Scorpio teaches us that in order to continue to grow, we need to let go of the things that are inhibiting us. That may mean changing our value system when the old one doesn't serve us any longer; knocking down our walls to build an addition, allowing more space for another to join; cutting off our dead branches or trimming roots that have rotted. Scorpio teaches us that sometimes strength can come from letting our boundaries down and standing in all of our vulnerability, taking whatever hits us. Through facing our fears, we become stronger. Sometimes we need to unground ourselves and let our subconscious waters show us what cannot be seen from above. Then we return to the surface with new meaning and power behind us. We have faced our fears and become stronger by doing so.

We always have to remember that death and suffering are a part of the human experience. In order to truly transform we need to undergo a death of sorts. It's essential to our evolution and is a part of the journey. There is no life without death. There is no light without a shadow. Embrace these moments of darkness we experience in ourselves and in our lives. They bring about the most growth, the most strength, and set us back on the path in alignment with our truth.

Everyone is so afraid of death, but the real Sufis just laugh: nothing tyrannizes their hearts. What strikes the oyster shell does not damage the pearl. ~ Rumi

Time for Reflection

We all have a darkness within us. We all have the power to penetrate our deep waters and resurface again.

What are you afraid of?

What are some of your secrets? What are the things you never tell others and don't even acknowledge yourself?

When do you do the dirty, internal work, diving into your own subconscious psyche? What is it that you find there?

When do you let go and become vulnerable with yourself? How about with someone else?

Time to get real with your intention and find out what it really means to you.

Strip away everything about this intention. What truths now lie at its core? What are you really seeking from its manifestation?

What scares you about your intention?

What if you lost everything you worked for on this intention so far? What would remain?

What are you willing to let go of, to allow to die within yourself in order to make room for this intention to be fully alive in your life?

How have your values changed and boundaries altered around this intention now that we've broken it down?

The call of death is the call of love. Death can be sweet if we answer it in the affirmative, if we accept it as one of the great eternal forms of life and transformation. ~ Herman Hesse

I am darkness.

There is a depth of meaning behind my existence.

My light and shadow are one in the same.

By opening myself up to the unknown, I receive glimpses of my source.

I find power through embracing the mystery.

Through a death within myself I am realigned with my truth.

I connect intimately with others by shedding layers of myself.

I swim in my dark, emotional waters and resurface fully transformed.

I am reborn.

Sagittarius

November 22nd ~ December 21st

Faith is the bird that feels the light when the dawn is still dark. ~ Rabindranath Tagore

Whew, we made it through Scorpio! That last phase was intense, going deep and getting real, doing all that dirty work that's necessary for our transformation. It's difficult and messy stuff to deal with. Now after all of that darkness, we have the opportunity to rise again with the power of the phoenix. It seems only fitting to soar high into the heavens with these new wings. It's the bow and arrow of Sagittarius that is going lead us forward on our path.

In Scorpio, we cleaned all the dirt that had accumulated on top of our worldly lens and now we have a whole new perspective. Sagittarius brings about the new awareness of our divinity and our relationship to the whole of life itself. Since discovering the possibility of life after death, what is our significance? Why did we choose to incarnate in this realm? These are the higher mind questions and thoughts that are in the conscious awareness of Sagittarius. From these questions, a new found sense of adventure is generated. If we're a part of this greater divinity and then we have a purpose to fulfill down here. Life must be one grand adventure to find our purpose and uncover its meaning. Sagittarius reminds us that we are here to find our way back to ourselves and rediscover why we're here. Within this stage we begin to grow our unwavering faith in the magic that is just beyond our perception waiting for us.

Through Sagittarius we are developing the overall story of our life that comes alive through our experiential growth. In order to create a great story, we need to have unforgettable experiences. Every experience, whether good or bad, is just another lesson to learn on our journey. Embedded within any story is a unique truth and teaching. Within the creation of our story we find what version of truth we embody. We become hungry students of life, constantly seeking out the answers to the universal questions and gathering new perspectives through which to see the world. From understanding different cultures and ways of living, we learn the different paths to truth and we begin to slowly piece together the grand meaning of it all.

Sagittarius is a mutable fire sign and is represented as the heat that radiates outward. We can't see it, but we can feel it as it dances far away from the source of the flame, altering all landscapes it moves through. Just as the heat is what allows us to sustain the bitter cold, our philosophy and faith is what will sustain us through the hardships in our lives. Our philosophical outlook is that bigger picture perspective. It's our guidebook, making sure we stay on the right path and align with our truth over the course of our life. Through Sagittarius we become conscious of this so we may alter our path if necessary.

Forms of Manifestation

Imagine the end of fall as we transition into winter. Traditionally, we would be preparing and bringing warmth into our homes. By this point, all the leaves have fallen from the trees, every branch bare. This is when the lovely evergreens stand out to us, nature's reminder that even in death, life remains.

Feel the warmth that radiates from Fire. Without that heat, surviving the cold moments in our life would be incredibly difficult. We can always create this warmth, and it will return again. It's a reminder that sustains us for our travels through darker and colder days.

Traveling to a far off land, to a place that's completely unfamiliar. There is a drastic perspective shift that comes from that sort of experience. We are immersed in another culture, opening our eyes to a totally new way of living in the world. By learning about all different cultural truths, we gain a better idea of what our truth might be.

The arrow that we shoot far off into the distance. Unsure of exactly where it landed, but we have the general sense of the direction it went. Now we begin the quest to find it! Who knows what kind of little experiences we'll encounter on the way! That's the whole adventure!

Our faith and our philosophy that we live by. Understanding that these are our arrows, acting as the bigger picture guide that we travel through life with.

Our joy and our ability to laugh at ourselves and not take life so seriously. Life seems more fun when we can embrace every experience as a lesson and an opportunity for growth.

Those times when we don't feel like we have a guiding philosophy, or maybe we're living someone else's truth. Or those times when we force our personal beliefs on another. We need to realize that there are many different paths to truth. We need to respect and allow others to walk their own paths and not be afraid to follow our own.

I don't know where I'm going but I'm on my way. ~ Carl Sagan

Integrating the Teachings

Life is all about the journey and we are the co-creators of what it's going to look like. The meaning of this existence is the experience. We are the only ones who can give meaning to our own lives. When we gain awareness of ourselves in the grander scheme of life, we develop a relationship with that. That's when we put ourselves in control of the myths and stories we enact and live out. We are the author, the pen is in our hand. Don't give that power to anyone else. This experience is about finding our own personal truth because at the end of the day, that's all we can really know. So just enjoy the ride of being human. If we mess up and make mistakes, whoops! No big deal, we learned something. We'll get another chance to try again!

We need to take our thoughts, the words we speak, and all of the information we flood our minds with (Gemini) and align them with our truth. Both the internal and external language that we use has an important place in the creation of our story. Words and thoughts are magical, they carry a vibrational pattern that we imprint on the energetic field around us. If we have a philosophy or a bigger picture idea of where we want to go with our life, we better make sure we are also "talking the talk" to help get us there. It's not enough to only have faith in something. We have to use language that aligns with that faith everyday. All of the language and information we are putting out and receiving each make up an individual stone on the greater path of our life.

In Aries we discovered who we are. Leo fueled that spark, showing us our heart, our power, and our creative ability. Sagittarius now brings in the deeper meaning. We become aware of our divinity as a spiritual being and our role as co-creator in this lifetime. Let's ignite the spark within us, fuel our flame, shine our light, and radiate our warmth far and wide. Let's create a story that reflects our innate beauty and the goodness that resides in each and every one of us. When we're in line with our truth and heart, we will no doubt create a beautiful story.

We don't receive wisdom; we must discover it for ourselves after a journey that no one can take for us or spare us. ~ Proust

Time for Reflection

We all have our stories to create in this crazy game of life. We are each our own archer with an arrow ready to aim wherever we choose.

What is your philosophy guiding you in this lifetime?

How do you radiate warmth, hope, and joy?

What is the story you wish to make out of your life here?

What is your truth, the greater meaning behind who you are?

What pushes you to travel far and wide? What are you seeking? What sustains you through the long, hard journeys?

Time to give this intention a deeper meaning. Let's incorporate it into the philosophy that drives your life.

How does this intention align with your truth?

What meaning does it give to your life? How does it aid in the creation of your story?

What direction is it leading you in?

How does your intention expand your perspective, giving you a bigger picture view of your life?

How have your thoughts or words changed now that you've grown a new perspective on this intention?

The purpose of life, after all, is to live it, to taste experience to the utmost, to reach out eagerly and without fear for newer and richer experience. ~ Eleanor Roosevelt

I AM MEANINGFUL.

I HAVE A RELATIONSHIP WITH MY LIFE AND THE PATH I AM WALKING.

THROUGH MY PHILOSOPHY I CREATE THE DIRECTION I AM HEADING.

I EMBODY ONE PATH TO TRUTH AND MY LIFE IS MY QUEST TO FIND IT.

EVERY EXPERIENCE IS A LESSON I HAVE ASKED FOR AND CAN LEARN FROM.

I HAVE FAITH THAT THERE IS A GREATER MEANING TO THIS EXISTENCE.

I OPEN MY AWARENESS AND SEE THE MAGIC THAT IS ALL AROUND US.

MY LIFE IS ABOUT THE EXPERIENCE.

I AM TRUTH.

Capricorn

December 22nd ~ January 19th

A man who dares to waste one hour of time, has not discovered the value of life. ~ Charles Darwin

We've traveled long distances to find our truth and create our story. We've set our sights high, aiming the arrow of our awareness far and wide with the knowledge that anything is possible. Unfortunately, no matter how high we shoot our arrow, at some point gravity's pull will bring it right back down to Earth. Sorry to have to burst our bubble, but now we are entering the reality of our harsh but wise teacher, Capricorn.

In Sagittarius we gained a whole new awareness to life and our relationship to it. As we enter the stage of Capricorn, we have to place that expansive awareness into a container. In this way, we learn of the limitations that are inherent to having a relationship to this earthly existence. There is a grand pattern and overall structure that encompasses our life cycle on this plane of reality. As a cardinal earth sign, Capricorn represents time as the initiating force that keeps the wheel of life spinning and binds us together in this realm. Through Capricorn, we begin to understand the ancient wisdom that can be found by following the natural cycle of time. In this way, traditions and ancestry are an important aspect of this stage. We can learn from the teachings passed down through many generations.

Since we have a limited amount of time here, Capricorn doesn't want us to waste a minute of it. We only have one human lifespan as this unique manifestation. Are we going to use our time and resources here wisely and efficiently? It is through these questions that we grow our body of responsibility; we develop an understanding that we have to be of service to this life that we now have a greater awareness of. If we are a part of a divine truth incarnated in human form, then we have to make something out of our time here. Capricorn wants us to make sure we have something concrete to show for ourselves at the end of our life. We have a responsibility to ourselves, to our fellow members of society, and to the Earth not to waste our divine power and build structures that will last for generations to come. Capricorn develops our ability to step up, stand strong, and take responsibility for who we are and what we create.

This stage of growth brings the understanding of all our own limitations that we carry with us. Realistically, what are the things we can and cannot do? We need to have a solid understanding of what we aren't capable of in order to direct our energy to the things we are actually good at. Because of this, Capricorn represents all of our accomplishments and achievements. The mountaintop of our lives, Capricorn is our legacy and what we are creating with our time here. The only way to build a solid legacy is by putting in time and hard work.

Forms of Manifestation

Imagine the beginning of winter and the entry into the coldest months of the year. Earth is barren and would seem almost lifeless if we were living away from civilization, out in nature as our ancestors did.

Picture the grandness of a mountain and the feelings that are invoked in you when in the presence of one. There is such majestic beauty held from their sheer size. We, too, have desires to be seen and remembered for all of time in that same way.

Now think of that same mountain, but imagine all of the incredibly hard work it would take to actually climb up the entire thing! It is no easy or quick task.

Look to the animal kingdom. Watch and observe how the animals are in sync with the rhythms and cycles of time and Earth.

Our karma and the things that we gathered in past lives that come back to limit us in some way. Our blood, our ancestors, and our DNA. From the moment we entered this reality, we were limited to a certain physical form.

The drive we feel when we set our sights on an achievement we wish to build. Putting in the time and hard work, not resting until we reach the top of the mountain. The pride that comes when we actually reach the top, when we can look back at all our work and know that we've built something solid.

The expectations we place on ourselves in order to accomplish certain things or act in a certain way. When we feel we have failed because of our limitations and feel we are not good enough. We need to realize that we are capable of mastering anything we wish. By understanding our limitations we become better equipped to accomplish our goals.

Let your life lightly dance on the edges of Time like dew on the tip of a leaf.
~ Rabindranath Tagore

Integrating the Teachings

Reality check: there are some things we just can't do, won't become, and will never accomplish. These lessons that Capricorn brings are harsh, but needed. It's only through understanding our own limitations that we can achieve the freedom we desire. By working with the tools we have been given and not wasting our time trying to be something we're not, we can focus all of our energy into using what we have at our disposal to create greatness! Honor and love your limitations, see them as gifts. Nature has been working within the cycles of limitations for generations. We can humble ourselves to this wisdom that the deep Earth carries as it operates within these wider arcs of time. We all carry karma, so let's accept it with grace and responsibility.

We always need to honor oppositions. While we are out mastering the objective world and our place in it, we need to remember where we came from, and honor the delicate inner world we carry within us everyday. By balancing out our inner subjective reality (Cancer) with the outer objective reality (Capricorn), we can develop a better mastery at navigating both worlds of our existence; one cannot exist without the other. Although there are certain responsibilities we might have and things we think we "need" to do, we have a responsibility to make sure our inner child feels safe and that our emotions are aligned with what we want to accomplish out in the world. If we continue to climb the mountain without watering or nurturing our inner world, then we aren't going to have lush or fulfilling landscapes to gaze back upon.

Through Capricorn we learn that good things take time, hard work, and diligence to build. To climb a mountain is not an easy task. If we want our Sagittarius truth to have a story it can remember and create, then we need to put in the work for it. Once we're at the mountaintop of our lives, we have the perspective of looking back and seeing everything we've gone through. We can see all of the challenges, accomplishments, and lessons that are learned by simply growing old and living life. It is this feeling of proud accomplishment that Capricorn hopes to bless us with.

...time is a companion who goes with us on the journey and reminds us to cherish each moment because they'll never come again. What we leave behind is not as important as how we've lived. ~ Captain Jean-Luc Picard

Time for Reflection

We have all limitations and boundaries that we have to work within. We are all capable of mastery.

What are the ways in which you see and feel yourself as limited?

Are these true limitations or ones you have placed on yourself?

How do you work within the boundaries you have been given in this life?

What do you consider yourself a master of? Or hope to achieve mastery of?

What wisdom are you hoping to gain from this lifetime? What is your legacy you wish to leave behind?

We want to make your intention worth something. Let's make it become a part of your legacy and grow to the highest mountain it can be.

What was the karma your intention carried with it? What are the limiting factors you've had to work through in order to sustain this intention?

How can you work with this intention in order to accomplish something?

Does this intention create any boundaries or limitations in yourself or your life? How can you work within those limitations?

How can you begin to master the integration of this intention within yourself?

How does your inner world feel now that your intention has grown and become more visible in the world?

The price of greatness is great responsibility. ~ Winston Churchill

I am responsible.

I am blessed with this life that I am not meant to waste.

I build greatness with my time here.

I step up and take responsibility for the actions I initiate.

I honor the earth and all of her ancient wisdom.

I respect all life forms with whom I share this cycle of time.

Through understanding my limitations I can accomplish anything.

I will reach my mountaintop, wherever I determine that to be.

I am capable of mastery.

I am limited and I have time.

Aquarius

January 20th ~ February 18th

Genius is the capacity to see ten things where the ordinary man sees one. ~ Ezra Pound

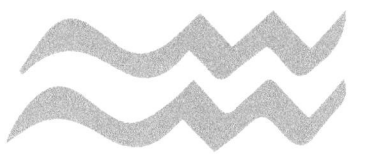

We've made it to the top of our mountains, hit our peaks, and have traveled as far as we possibly can within this reality. Where then, do we go from here? It doesn't make much sense for us to just isolate ourselves at the top of the mountain. The next logical step would be to explore those places we can't see, traveling to the space just beyond the boundaries of reality. It is within this unseen realm that we tap into the energy of Aquarius.

What is it that lies just beyond the confines of reality, untouched by the laws of nature and time? It is the ever curious nature of the mind that takes us out of the world we thought we knew and taps into a place of wider consciousness. The archetype of Aquarius embodies this otherworldly space where we find the universal mind. Here is where we discover the full power and capacity of the mind as the messenger and traveler between realms. In this stage of development, we begin to intellectually conceptualize thoughts that are outside our ordinary realm of understanding and integrate these thoughts into our earthly lives. We are breaking free of our earthly constraints, stepping outside of ourselves and our individual consciousness, and learning to see the world from a collective perspective.

A fixed air sign found within the still vastness of outer space, Aquarius represents the open and forward thinking mind, and the condensing of that limitless knowledge back down into the Earth. The growth we experience when on an Aquarian vibration allows us to think outside of the box, tap into the collective mind, and perceive and understand innovative new ideas never before brought down into this reality. We break free of the limits found in Capricorn, as they are seen as a box for our global mind which continually seeks to break physical boundaries.

One of Aquarius's earthly embodiments is our communities. When we become more conscious of the connection we share in the ethers, we can shift our perspective to more of a community-based mentality. Think of all the progress that can be made for humanity as a whole if we are operating from that mindset. If we put multiple creative minds together on a common goal and idea, they become stronger. Aquarius also has a keen desire for individual freedom within communities. Always seeking the best way to improve human life far into the future, Aquarius understands the importance of giving individuals the freedom to creatively pursue their own unique paths and interests. Everyone benefits when new creations, art, and technology can come to life. Through Aquarius, we come to know that we are all unique and individual manifestations of the divine. We all carry the ability to tap into ideas and realms that are greater than just our individual selves.

Forms of Manifestation

Imagine the middle of winter; a time when we aren't actively doing things outside, so we have the opportunity to explore the realms of our ideas. We are beginning to set goals for the year ahead. Traditionally, this is the time when you look to your community for assistance in the harsh winter.

Picture the vastness of outer space. We cannot see it from our view here on Earth, and in a way it is foreign to us. When we open our minds to exploration we find that there is so much more out there to learn and discover, even more than what our limited minds can grasp.

The mad scientist. Someone who nobody understands and is not recognized in his time. He was thinking too far into the future to be understood.

Our communities. A group of individuals coming together with common goals, tapping into similar ideas and expressing them through different outlets. Think of how much more evolved and developed an idea can become when multiple minds are working on its manifestation rather than just one.

Our inventiveness. Those times when we are thinking outside of the box of our limitations. When we gain a new perspective and see an idea that has never been created before, impacting humanity's growth as a whole.

Our uniqueness and individuality, wanting to stand out from the crowd. Or our feelings of isolation that can stem from that. When we feel different from the group, like an outcast that is alienated. We need to realize that there is a specialness to our individuality. There's a whole world full of people who are different than us and who might not like us for our uniqueness. If we can maintain our integrity and stay true to ourselves, we will no doubt find a community of people that is accepting of who we are.

Let us love winter, for it is the spring of genius. ~ Pietro Aretino

Integrating the Teachings

When operating through its highest potential, Aquarius can teach us all of the good that can come from intelligence and our human mind. When we can dial in our focus and put our mind to conscious work, its transcendent ability will shine through. The mind is a tool that allows us to traverse all realms, looking back into the past and far into the future. Through Aquarius's teachings we can mindfully work to evolve ourselves, our species, and our life as a whole.

In order for us to integrate the untapped knowledge we learn from Aquarius, we need to remember the teachings of its opposition (Leo) and bring that knowledge back down into the heart. We need to ground it and center it within our place of connectedness here on Earth. What's the point of having a genius mind if not to bring that universal wisdom back to humanity. In this way, we are stepping into the mind's true role as being in service to the heart, then our innovations will come from a place of love for all of creation. It is our heart which tethers us to this world so we don't get too lost in our minds.

Aquarius teaches us that our uniqueness is in line with a higher purpose, and we begin to fully understand what it means to be an individual. Yes, we come from and can access this pool of collective consciousness, but look at the multitude of ways that consciousness expresses itself on this plane of reality. We each have the ability to become and create something that has never existed before. The ability to bring universal wisdom down into our hearts, makes that wisdom special and unique to us. Our version of that truth only adds to the wholeness.

All men are caught in an inescapable network of mutuality, tied in a single garment of destiny. Whatever affects one directly affects all indirectly. I can never be what I ought to be until you are what you ought to be, and you can never be what you ought to be until I am what I ought to be. ~ Martin Luther King, Jr

Time for Reflection

We all have a uniqueness and we all have the ability to tap into our wider and greater consciousness.

What makes you authentically unique?

In what ways do you break boundaries and barriers?

What kind of community do you like to surround yourself with?

When do you think outside of the box? How do you give yourself that sort of perspective?

What brings you into a more collective mindset? How do you tap into that unseen realm?

Let's begin to think about that intention with a wider lens and from a separate perspective.

How does this intention add to your uniqueness?

In what ways does it connect you to a concept that is greater than your individual self?

When you are living authentically within your intention, how will that unique manifestation add to the betterment of humanity as a whole?

How can you share with your community the wisdom you have learned from healing with this intention?

Now that you have a greater understanding of this intention, how does it feel when you bring it back into your heart?

I am not eccentric. It's just that I am more alive than most people. I am an unpopular electric eel set in a pond of catfish. ~ Edith Sitwell

I am unique.

I see beyond my limitations and constraints.

My mind allows me to tap into the wider collective consciousness.

I am connected to a web that is bigger than my individual self.

I condense innovative ideas down into this reality.

My outside of the box perspective aids in humanity's evolution.

My uniqueness has a place in the greater wholeness of life.

I am one of a myriad of forms of universal consciousness.

I am liberated.

Pisces

February 19th ~ March 20th

In one drop of water are found all the secrets of all the oceans. ~ Kahlil Gibran

Now that we've tapped into this realm of the unseen and understand the concept of a collective consciousness, what does the final stage of our journey entail for us? It's not enough to just understand the concept of unity, now we need to become it. It's another thing entirely to embody unity in everything we do and to feel it throughout our whole essence. It is within this vast feeling of connectedness that we find the ocean realm of Pisces.

All water signs embody the nature of feeling, and in Pisces we begin to embody all the serenity that encompasses the feeling of completion. On the layer of our emotional body, this is seen as our capacity to feel universal compassion and forgiveness. We are at home now; our cycle of evolution through this specific journey is now finished. Whatever happened during our time spent here - whatever grew and developed, whoever we hurt or hurt us - there's no changing any of it. So it's better to come to a place of acceptance and forgiveness for each part. We can begin to hold compassion in our hearts for each stage of our journey when we embrace that. Pisces opens up our senses in order to see the greater lesson behind all of it. All of the mistakes and achievements, all of the joys and sorrows, those are pieces of this journey that made us who we are now.

In order to truly feel this connectedness, all boundaries need to dissolve. Pisces allows us to finally experience this feeling when all things begin to disintegrate. It is within these liminal spaces of existence where all boundaries cease to be, that all things merge into one. There is no more separation. We remember where we came from and the truth of who we really are. Through Pisces we begin to feel this way in relation to all of creation, and it's hard not to come from a place of compassion in everything we do. Pisces is a mutable water sign, changeable and shifting, yet in each form the true essential nature and spirit remains. It is within this stage that we begin to truly embrace change and the shifting tides that life offers. We have to be able to surrender to the greater movement of this universal spirit if we want to harmonize with the dance of life.

Pisces is the beginning and the end; the Alpha and the Omega; everything and nothing embodied in stillness and movement at the same time. So not only are we at the end of our journey, but we are also at the start of one. In Pisces we find the magical realm where all things begin, the space of visions and dreams. Everything that we see manifest here in this reality began as a dream or a vision and was then brought down into this physical existence. Remember that place of stillness we inhabited before we began? All things come from that place of prayer and all things return to it. Pisces is the universal spirit that we all came from and are all a part of.

Forms of Manifestation

Imagine the end of winter transitioning into spring. The snow is slowly dissolving and we begin to see grass again. There is a lightness that we can feel and see within all things as the anticipation of new life is returning once again.

Picture the vastness and serenity of a still ocean. Place yourself way out in the middle of one, allowing it to surround all of you. There is no land in sight and as you gaze upon the faint horizon line, it's almost as if the ocean and sky are merging into one.

Think of the nature of Water with the ability to shift forms and yet still exist as Water in each one. Imagine the beauty of the Water cycle, evaporating from the Earth, merging and dissolving into the clouds and raining back down again. We all drink the same Water, as did our ancestors and so will our children. It is the spirit that weaves through our past, present, and future.

Envision a foggy day. Everything that can be seen in front of you is gray mist, nothing is distinguishable. Yet, it is not quite tangible, and you can glide right through it; the picture of what's in front you slowly becomes more clear.

Our dreams and imagination, the space of our visions; magical realms that can seem so real and yet sometimes so intangible when we return to reality.

Our prayers and those moments when we truly feel and embody our connection to a higher divine power. As if spirit has entered the space we are in and dissolved itself into our hearts.

Our escapism and those times we don't want to live within this plane of reality, it's just too hard. The desire to just float away into nothingness. When we drift too far away into our imagination and our dreams, avoiding the work and responsibilities that come with separation. We need to understand that this place actually doesn't serve us, and in order to really feel that peace, we have to bring it down into our earthly selves as it does not exist separate from that.

Birth is not the beginning. Death is not the end. ~ Chuang Tsu

Integrating the Teachings

Pisces is the true teacher of what it means to surrender. The lessons within this energy show us how to release, let go, and accept the natural flow of life. Pisces enables us to feel and fully embody our spiritual nature. Maintaining the health of that layer of ourselves is just as important as the maintenance of our physical health. When we are in tune with our spirit and we feel the connection with the rest of life, we can find serenity and radiate compassion.

With the merging of Pisces together with Virgo, we learn to walk the spiritual path with earthly feet. In this way, we can bring intention into every act we do, infusing spirit into all of our earthly services. This veil of separation that Virgo brings is just that - a veil. If we can learn to see and feel the divinity that connects us all underneath, then we'll begin to experience a deeper healing for ourselves and our planet. It's about shifting our perspective to see all the "chaos" in our life as a part of the divine order.

In Pisces we become disillusioned of our separations. There is no difference between the beginning and the end, the cycle always continues to spin. There are no division lines and no oppositions. All of these individual energies and forces we learned about are constantly changing, merging, and dancing with one another. Each of them flow between all layers of all things, interweaving into the others and back out again. We are just as multifaceted as they are. We interact and dance in the same way, both with them and with all things.

Pisces shares with us the unity we can find within the dance of life. Once we reach a state of unity, life force energy is going to want to move again; such is the nature of the dance. It wants to become separate yet again, causing disorder and chaos and then makes the journey back home. Now that we have this perspective of how the whole cycle flows, we can work to bring this connectedness into everything we do. We know that no matter what happens, everything always ends, and begins, in this space. We truly find our peace when we can learn to find stillness even in the midst of movement within the chaos.

Everything that has a beginning has an end. Make your peace with that and all will be well.
~ Buddha

Time for Reflection

We are all connected. We all have the ability to feel and embody compassion and universal love. We are all visionary.

How do you embody compassion?

How do you find peace and serenity? When do you feel whole and at home?

When life seems in total chaos, how do you find the quiet stillness within it all?

How do you make time for prayer? What does your spiritual practice look like?

How do you work with your imagination, visions, and dreams?

It's time to become what it is you intended. Let's bring this intention home.

Have you found peace with this intention? Does it bring you a sense of serenity?

How does it feel to have this intention boundless within your existence?

What new visions do you receive from sitting in the feeling of completion with this intention?

How can you bring this intention into your everyday earthly healing?

How can you embody it in everything you are? Can it weave itself into everything you do?

Doesn't it feel like it's been a part of you this entire time, you just had to remember it….?

Eternity: I am drawn to the wild edge of the ocean of my being. My curiosity unbound, I test the limits of the limitless and the boundaries of the timeless. I walk the path, the way, the way of ways to the end which is not an end. ~ Jonathan Lockwood Huie

I am dissolving.

The same spirit that runs through me, runs through all of creation.

I feel the connectedness that is woven throughout life.

I am visionary and can embody the stillness found in unity.

My imagination and dreams are ways that spirit speaks to me.

I find forgiveness and acceptance for myself and others.

I am boundless and merge into universal love.

I embody compassion.

I am whole.

We are one

FROM A PLACE OF STILLNESS, A VISION IGNITES A SINGLE SPARK...

ARIES ~ Awakening of a new consciousness.
TAURUS ~ Grounding into physicality and form.
GEMINI ~ Development of language and thinking process.
CANCER ~ Discovery of reflective nature through feelings.
LEO ~ Creative expression of the fully embodied self.
VIRGO ~ Working the self into an earthly existence and healing separateness.

LIBRA ~ Need for balance through oppositions and change in direction.
SCORPIO ~ Descent into darkness and transformation through releasing.
SAGITTARIUS ~ Expansion of perspective through finding higher meaning and purpose.
CAPRICORN ~ Understanding earthly limitations and reaching highest accomplishments.
AQUARIUS ~ Tapping into the realm beyond the seen reality for collective evolution.
PISCES ~ Dissolving all boundaries of separation and returning home to stillness.

AND THE CYCLE CONTINUES....

The spiritual journey involves going beyond hope and fear, stepping into unknown territory, continually moving forward. The most important aspect of being on the spiritual path may be just to keep moving. ~ Pema Chodron

That my friends, completes this rotation through of a never-ending cycle.

Wholeness. An entire journey of manifestation, realization, integration, and release has now occurred.

But it doesn't end here with these pages. The wheel of life is always in motion and continues to spin. I hope that within the place of visions and stillness we just ended on, a new spark was ignited in your soul.

Take these teachings with you as you move forward with a new intention and walk with them throughout the rest of your life. Continue to grow in your relationship with these powerful forces. They will continue to guide you on a path that is in harmonious resonance with nature. These cycles are happening all around us, all the time, and in a multitude of different manifestations. Embrace them and work with them on all levels of your life.

Return to these pages when you need guidance. You have placed a piece of your heart into these mandalas. They will help remind you the way home when you feel lost. Come back to the reflection questions, as your answers may change as you continue to grow. Work through this guided process with any new intention you wish to develop within yourself.

I hope you have discovered new things about yourself through this journey. I hope your intention has grown and evolved in some way, and dissolved itself back into your very essence. I hope you have found peace.

It's been an honor to have walked with you through this journey.

Love & Gratitude

*May all beings everywhere
with whom we are inseparably connected,
be fulfilled, awakened, liberated and free.
May there be peace in this world
and throughout the entire universe,
and may we all together
complete the spiritual journey.*

~ Lama Surya Das

Space for Reflections

Fill your paper with the breathings of your own heart. ~ William Wordsworth

Space for Reflections

All that we are is the result of what we have thought. ~ Buddha

A little more about the heart and soul behind this book:

Megan Ryan Walsh began her self-healing journey about five years ago. The path of coming home to her heart has led her into a deeper connection with nature. The language of astrology became the way she would learn to hear the teachings of nature. With the heart of a Sagittarius, she went on a quest to find the her truth within these teachings and studied endlessly on her own for quite some time. She eventually became an apprentice with astrologer Tyler Penor, based in Washington, and studied under his guidance during a year long program. She also became a student of the School of Evolutionary Herbalism based in Oregon, learning how to weave the medicine of plants together with astrology in order to invoke healing on a much deeper level.

Through her newfound love for these healing modalities, she co-founded Inner Mandala Medicine with her soul sister, Lyz Krieger. Beginning as a blog, IMM blossomed into a healing community, connecting people to their own inner mandala by giving them the healing tools they resonate with.

Dancing as a professional ballet dancer in Chicago for twelve years, creating beauty and art has always been an extremely important part of Megan's life. Integrating her love for astrology and art has been an incredible healing process for her soul growth. Ultimately, she wishes to share these teachings with others and spread beauty throughout the world.

Since the self-healing path is a never-ending one, Megan embraces the ongoing journey she's embarked on and hopes to continue to share her lessons and experiences along the way.

Interested in diving further into your astrological knowledge? Start by working with your own natal chart! Megan offers a selection of astrology consultations and coaching if you need help getting started.

Visit innermandalamedicine.com if you're called to work with these cycles on a deeper and more personal level. Check out all the other healing services and content we offer!

Inner Mandala Medicine

Change your energy, change our life.